© 2020, Arnaud BOCHURBERG

Edition :

BoD – Books on Demand

12/14 Rond point des Champs-Elysées – 75008 Paris

Impression : Bod – Books on Demand, Norderstedt, Allemagne

Illustrations and layout : Charlotte SOUPLET

ISBN : 978-2-3222-0534-9

All rights reserved.

No part of this publication may be reproduced, stored in a retrieval system, stored in a database and / or published in any form or by any means, electronic, mechanical, photocopying, recording or otherwise, without the prior written permission of the publisher.

Legal deposit : *april 2020*

READ
THIS BOOK AND
BOOST
YOUR
CONFIDENCE
IN
30 MINUTES

FROM THE SAME AUTHOR

"**The mind, the key to performance**", *Arnaud Bochurberg, Ed. Cithéa, © 2010*

"**Make the impossible possible**", *Preface by the President of the French Republic Emmanuel Macron, Karl Olive and Arnaud Bochurberg, Ed. Balland, © 2018*

"**Asserting oneself in all serenity**", *Com Comedy Challenge, Arnaud Bochurberg and Maxime Chesnais, Ed. Le Souffle d'Or, © 2019*

To all those who have given me confidence, to those who have inspired me, and to those who have encouraged me to pass it on.

" If you have self confidence, you will inspire confidence in others." Goethe

SUMMARY

Introduction	7-9
Context	10-13

CHAPTER I - INITIALIZING THE SYSTEM

Identify files to be trashed.	33
Trashing	47

CHAPTER II - SETTING UP THE NEW OPERATING SYSTEM

Multifaceted perception Program	58-71
Intra personal resources Program	72-77
Program to induce posture as the origin of self-confidence	73-83
Self coaching Program	84-95
Program to make peace with your fears	96-116

CHAPITRE III - SETTING UP AN ANTIVIRUS PROGRAM

Conclusion	120

ARE YOU
READY?

INTRODUCTION

When I was a young teacher at the University, I was given the task of preparing students for entrance exams to the top-ranking business schools.

I remember how enthusiastic I was, passing on an abundance of energy, and boldly claiming : *"you can do it"*, *"you have to believe in yourself"*, *" Be self-confident and you will succeed! »*

A student came to me at the end of my speech and simply asked me, *"You're telling us that we have to be self-confident. But how do we do that? »*

The question was simple enough. However I spent the next few seconds speechless. I realized that I was asking them to reach the top of the mountain with self-affirmations without giving them the proper tools. I wasn't showing them the way.

INTRODUCTION

That was the moment when I started work on finding the keys to guide them on the road to :

SELF-CONFIDENCE

I invite you to walk this path with me by reading this book and taking up this challenge to boost your confidence in 30 minutes.

CONTEXT

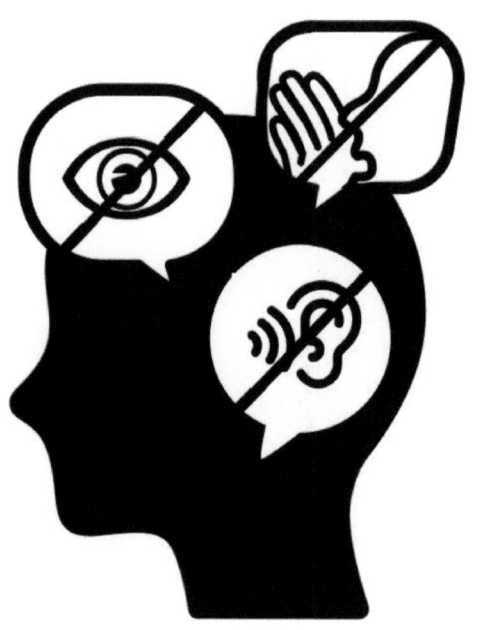

CONTEXT

We *are afraid of* **EVERYTHING**.

When we were born, we were **FEARLESS.**

Over the years, we stored up all the « little voices » in our heads that eventually became
PARALYZING BARRIERS.

We were born with confidence, then little by little we lost it due to outside influences. It needs to be re-identified in order to change our operating system.

OBJECTIVE :
DARE TO SUCCEED

DARE TO SUCCEED

« This is not because things are tough that we don't dare to do them, it's because we don't dare to do things that they are tough. » - Seneca

If we want to succeed and gain confidence, we need to live new experiences to get out of our comfort zone and become at ease in situations we are not familiar with.

Getting out of your comfort zone means making new connections -expanding your territory - finding yourself comfortable where others are uncomfortable.

> To succeed, **we must dare to cross the fears that surround our comfort zone and learn new skills.**

OBJECTIVE

" *Once upon a time there was a King who had two problems : his daughter and his fortune.*

His daughter was so beautiful that the King could not chose who he would marry her to, especially since the suitor would also inherit his considerable fortune.

So he decided to invite all the suitors : the rich, the poor, the beautiful, the ugly…
He organized a big reception in his palace.
A crowd of people showed up. A show was put on.

In the middle of the evening, the King spoke :
« You know why you are here. I wish to marry my daughter to someone who can take good care of her and inherit my fortune. To this end, I invite you all to join me around the pool. »

A hundred suitors gathered around a large pool as the King had requested. The pool was without light while the King indicated the rules of the game.
« The first one to cross the pool from one end to the other shall have my daughter and my fortune. I have to tell you that in the water there are sharks, crocodiles, hungry piranhas. The water is dark and you'll have to get out alive. »

OBJECTIVE

« At the King's announcement, no one feels brave enough to go into the water. Everyone calls the King a fool.

All of a sudden, everyone hears a SPLASH and all heads turn to a guy who starts swimming with all his might, and in less than 50 seconds he comes out the other side completely out of breath.

The King approaches him and says « Congratulations, you have won my daughter and my fortune ! You are the only one who had the courage to face your own fear because I tell you, there were in fact neither piranhas, nor crocodiles, nor sharks in the water. So, young man, what drove you to throw yourself into the water ? »

At that moment, the young man says, « Well, I'd like to know who pushed me into the water so I can thank him. »

OBJECTIVE

DARE TO SUCCEED

Usually, we don't move away from our comfort zone because we think it will mean having to face our fears (fear of failure, fear of the people look, etc...)

As shown in the illustration above, by **moving out of the comfort zone** and crossing the fear zone into the training zone (where skills are learned), we finally reach the success zone, which will, in turn, become a new comfort zone.

STRATEGY :

INITIALIZE OUR OPERATING SYSTEM

AND REPLACE IT WITH A NEW SYSTEM

PART 1

INITIALIZE
OUR OPERATING
SYSTEM

PART 1 INITIALIZE OUR OPERATING SYSTEM

Mission 1 :

IDENTIFY *FILES* TO BE **TRASHED**.

IN OUR BRAINS :

New = DANGER
New = PAIN

We're looking within our comfort zone instead of looking beyond it.

PART 1 INITIALIZE OUR OPERATING SYSTEM

A man, in the middle of the night, is looking for his keys under a lamppost. A passer-by asks him where he thinks he lost them.

The man points to a remote location in the darkness.

« Why don't you look for them over there then ? » asks the stanger.
« Because this is where the light is ! » responds the man.

Yet, it is in the darkness, in the uncertainty, that the answers to our questions are often found.

IDENTIFY YOUR **FEARS** TO FIND OUT WHAT *PREVENTS YOU* FROM TRUSTING YOURSELF.

- Afraid of public speaking?
- Afraid you're not up to it?
- Afraid of failing?
- Afraid of disappointing ?
- Afraid of what other people think of you?
- Fear of being rejected by family and friends?
- Fear of being criticized?
- Fear of taking chances?
- Fear of being humiliated?
- Fear of daring?

PART 1 INITIALIZE OUR OPERATING SYSTEM

WHAT ARE THE **NEGATIVE THOUGHTS** ASSOCIATED WITH THESE FEARS THAT *UNDERMINE* **CONFIDENCE**?

When your pessimistic inner voice tells you things like :

« You can't make it, you're gonna fail... »

« You're not up to it. »

« No one is interested in what you're saying. »

« What you're saying is uninteresting. »

« You look ridiculous. »

« You're gonna disappoint them. »

PART 1 INITIALIZE OUR OPERATING SYSTEM

Write down on the chart below each of your fears and the negative thought associated with this fear :

Chart of fears

FEAR	ASSOCIATED NEGATIVE THOUGHT

LOCATE THE *ROOTS* OF YOUR **INSECURITY** THAT *UNDERMINE* YOUR SELF-CONFIDENCE

Think about the things that keep you from moving forward.

What makes you feel sad or gives you a feeling of being inferior?
Is it :

- A traumatic experience?

- A relationship that ended badly?

- A painful adolescence?

PART 1 INITIALIZE OUR OPERATING SYSTEM

Write down all the things that hold you back on the chart below.

Chart of shadows

INSECURITY LIST
What makes you sad :
• -------------------------------   • -------------------------------
What makes you feel inferior :
• -------------------------------   • -------------------------------
A traumatic experience :
• -------------------------------   • -------------------------------

LOCATE THE *REASONS* FOR YOUR SHYNESS

Think about the things that keep you from moving forward.

- What causes shyness for you ?

- Which situations cause shyness ?

- What do you think about when you feel shy?

PART 1 INITIALIZE OUR OPERATING SYSTEM

Write down all the things which cause shyness and the associated thought on the chart below :

Chart of the roots of shyness

SITUATION CAUSING SHYNESS	ASSOCIATED THOUGHT

> By looking at this chart, you are able to assess for yourself whether your emotional responses are justified and whether they are proportionate to the situation encountered.

THE FIRST THING TO DO :

1. *Identify these fears, the thoughts associated with them, the roots of your insecurity, the reasons for your shyness.*

2. *Recognize them as negative, do not push them away.*

3. *Acknowledge and accept that they are useless.*

By facing your fears, you will no longer be invaded by them to the point of being paralyzed...

THE SECOND THING TO DO :

DISTINGUISH WHAT WE ARE FROM WHAT WE THINK...

Take a step back !

PART 1 INITIALIZE OUR OPERATING SYSTEM

Mission 2 :

TRASHING *THE FILES*

METHOD 1

« Thank you, but I don't agree anymore... »

To break free, one must detach from these stubborn, internalized thoughts.

As the following story shows :

« Sulky was a young wild horse captured at the age of two. Destined to be sold, he had to be tamed first. It was decided to tie Sulky up with a rope and a stake planted in the ground. The animal couldn't bear his condition and desperately tried to get loose by screaming, biting the rope, hitting the stake with his hind legs. But to no avail, the rope was strong and thick and the stake was firmly planted in the ground. Suddenly, one morning, Sulky decided to give up, stopped hind feet tapping, yelling, and biting the rope. His master decided that day to set him free. Sulky wasn't sold because he was doing to his master extraordinary favors and he wouldn't let go.»

You're sometimes like Sulky. " Your thoughts " is the rope, " the object of your annoyance ", the stake in the ground.
<u>To detach yourself from your thoughts, you have to let them be and attach yourself to another mental representation</u>. Indeed, when you focus your thoughts on avoiding your worries in order to prevent the suffering of thinking about them, you strengthen them even more.

A negative thought is sometimes a protection against adversity. It is better to welcome it, observe it, and say :

« Thank you, but I don't agree anymore... »

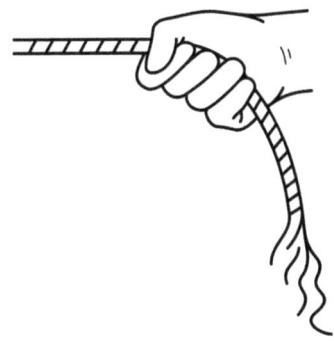

METHOD 2

Getting rid of misrepresentations

How do you symbolically get rid of all the things that keep holding you back ?

- **The objective :** To free yourself from difficult, painful experiences in your life by relieving you of the associated negative emotions that block your self-confidence.

- **The instructions :** Read aloud the charts of **FEARS**, **INSECURITIES**, and the roots of **SHYNESS**. You pronounce all the words without anger or sadness, trying to be as neutral as possible, as if you were reading the text of an author you don't know.

- **Unburden hostile emotions :** You can burn these outlines or tear them into pieces.

By getting rid of these charts, you are making a resolution to leave these representations behind.

TO ERASE NEGATIVE THOUGHTS

You have to think about something else instead of trying not to think about it.

Indeed, the mind is not capable of thinking about the negation of something. For example, if I tell you, "Don't think about an apple", guess what ? You just thought of it. To avoid thinking about something negative, it is useless to tell yourself not to think about it. **You have to try to think about something else.**

Here's a **metaphorical tale** that illustrates why you shouldn't think about the worst and why you should think positively.

> *A very tired traveler sat in the shade of a tree without suspecting that he had just found a magic tree, «the Tree of Wishes». Sitting on the hard ground, he thought it would be nice to be in a soft bed. Immediately, a bed appeared next to him.*

Surprised, the man sat down and said that the height of happiness would be reached if a young girl would come in and massage his crooked legs. A girl appeared and massaged him very pleasantly.

« I'm hungry, » said the man, « and eating right now would certainly be a delight. ». A table emerges, loaded with succulent food. The man enjoyed himself. He ate and drank. His head was spinning a little. His eyelids, under the influence of the wine and fatigue, were drooping.

He let himself go all the way to the bed, still thinking of the marvelous events of that extraordinary day. « I will sleep for an hour or two » he thought to himself. The worst thing would be if a tiger came by while I was sleeping. »

A tiger immediately appeared and devoured him.

Think about it...**Thinking about the worst is often what devours you.**

TO GET RID OF THE BURDENS OF THE PAST...

Imagine that you are running your life as a blimp.

Imagine that you put negative thoughts that have always blocked your confidence in ballast bags.

You're slowly climbing up in the air...

You take one of these bags and you throw it overboard.

You find that you're lighter and the ball takes you higher.

You take another bag and throw it overboard... you climb up again.

PART 1 INITIALIZE OUR OPERATING SYSTEM

You just got rid of the weight of the past that was pulling you down…

PART 2

SETTING UP THE NEW OPERATING SYSTEM

MULTIFACETED PERCEPTION SOFTWARE

We interpret everything that we see, hear and feel.

The events of our lives are not at the origin of our emotions but the perception we have of these events.

Our emotions therefore depend on our perceptual filters.

Life can be thought of as **a multi-sided dice.**

Each situation can be perceived in different ways.

Think about it : to change your prism, isn't it enough to find the angle that suits you better ?

PART 2 SETTING UP THE NEW OPERATING SYSTEM

Example :
You miss a job interview. You perceive this failure as a catastrophe because you had put everything on this interview and think that you will not find anything else.

→ **You can also see another side of the dice** by telling yourself that if you didn't get the job, it wasn't right for you and that this situation will lead you in a more interesting direction...

MULTIFACETED PERCEPTION SOFTWARE

Turning events into opportunities, turning negative into positive.

What we believe is the fruit of what we have stored.

The Brain is an organ subject to the laws of plasticity. It is an "interpreting machine" capable of transforming what is negative into positive and even capable of transforming, why not, **fear** into opportunity.

Often, it is the fear represented in our minds that is actually arousing the **FEAR.**

PART 2 SETTING UP THE NEW OPERATING SYSTEM

FEAR is a fantasized and erroneous appreciation of reality, isn't it ?

FANTASIZED

ERRONEOUS

APPRECIATION of

REALITY

MULTIFACETED PERCEPTION SOFTWARE

Change the way you look at things :

Instead of telling yourself :

"Is it 100% **POSSIBLE**?"

Ask yourself the question :

" Is it 100% **IMPOSSIBLE**?"

PART 2 SETTING UP THE NEW OPERATING SYSTEM

If it's not 100% **_IMPOSSIBLE_**,

Then it's somehow **POSSIBLE**

MULTIFACETED PERCEPTION SOFTWARE

Instead of telling yourself :

" Will 100% of people **LIKE IT ?** *"*

Ask yourself the question :

" Will 100% of people **HATE IT ?"**

PART 2 SETTING UP THE NEW OPERATING SYSTEM

If it's not 100% of people who are going to hate it...

Then somehow **YOU ARE GOING TO INSPIRE <u>AT LEAST ONE PERSON</u>**

PART 2 SETTING UP THE NEW OPERATING SYSTEM

YOU DON'T JUST HAVE TO BELIEVE IN IT TO GET THERE.

YOU JUST HAVE TO KEEP BELIEVING.

MULTIFACETED PERCEPTION SOFTWARE

Challenge your negative thoughts that undermine self-confidence

Once you have identified your negative thoughts (influenced by your emotions), ask yourself :

" Why can't I realize this? I can do it ! "

" I have the skills to do it because I've already done new or difficult things."

" There is no reason why I can't do it this time! "

MULTIFACETED PERCEPTION SOFTWARE

Replace negative thoughts with positive ones.

Here are some examples of substitution:

Negative Thinking	Positive Thinking
I'm not up to it	Who sets the height? I'm going to lower the level of my goals to be able to achieve them
I'm not gonna make it	I'm not a fortune teller. I'll stop guessing. My positive thoughts turn into positive experiences

PART 2 SETTING UP THE NEW OPERATING SYSTEM

Negative Thinking	Positive Thinking
What happens if I fail?	I'm thinking about the game and not the stakes. I replace a doubt « will I succeed ? » with a procedure « I know what to do, I know how to do it and this, I know I can do it »
Everyone's gonna find my intervention bad	I'm not looking to be loved by everyone but to inspire at least one person
I'm afraid to fail.	«*I never lose, either I win or I learn*» N. Mandela « *Success is going from failure to failure without losing your enthusiasm.* » W. Churchill
I'm afraid I'm making a mistake.	"*The greatest mistake a man can make is to be afraid to make one...*" Elbert Hubbard

INTRAPERSONAL RESOURCES SOFTWARE

Cultivate victories

We observe that our past positive experiences strengthen our identity

Our coherence is often in line with
what we believe we are.

Ex : If I think I'm generous

→ I will behave as such

PART 2 SETTING UP THE NEW OPERATING SYSTEM

INTRAPERSONAL RESOURCES SOFTWARE

Build your library of positive representations

Neuroscience has discovered that the **same areas** of the brain are activated **when you do** something as **when you imagine doing** something...

So, if as much good happens to you as bad, but you only focus on the negative, you will sincerely feel like your life is full of failures.

Take back the control over your mind !...

...until it has returned to the path of positivity :

make the effort to often think about all the good things that happened to you, especially when you have successfully stepped out of your comfort zone.

PART 2 SETTING UP THE NEW OPERATING SYSTEM

On this board you will place images of you and the life you dream of.

The subconscious mind works as a computer.

→ *If you program it with negative thoughts, it will provide you with negative experiences.*

INTRAPERSONAL RESOURCES SOFTWARE

Here are a few examples from well-known personalities to inspire us...

✔ **Kicked off his basketball team for being too bad :**

➤ *Michael Jordan*

✔ **Rejected 30 times by publishers who tell her that her book is inadmissible :**

➤ *Joanne Rowling (Harry Potter)*

PART 2 SETTING UP THE NEW OPERATING SYSTEM

✔ *Refused 3 times from a cinema school because he didn't have the potential of a director :*

➤ *Steven Spielberg*

✔ *Fired from his newspaper for lack of imagination :*

➤ *Walt Disney*

✔ *His singing teachers advised him not to sing because he has neither the size, the voice nor the culture :*

➤ *Charles Aznavour*

PROGRAM TO INDUCE THE POSTURE AT THE SOURCE OF SELF-CONFIDENCE

Posture
Breathing
Smile

If the lack of confidence is acting on the body :

✓ *I'm scared* ➤ *I'm not behaving well.*

✓ *I'm scared* ➤ *I can't breathe.*

✓ *I'm scared* ➤ *I don't smile at myself.*

...The body reacts to self-confidence.

PROGRAM TO INDUCE POSTURE AS THE ORIGIN OF SELF-CONFIDENCE

Seeking to "become" instead of "having"

There is a misconception that trust is a matter of experiences nourished by positive situations stored up in our lives.

<u>But self-confidence should be unconditional</u>, it means daring to do something unknown, regardless of one's past experience, realizing that we have the right resources to do so.

Becoming aware that everything that happens to us...helps us to grow...

PART 2 SETTING UP OF THE NEW OPERATING SYSTEM

A simple questioning sometimes opens up positive ways :

✓ **What would I do if I was confident?**

✓ **What would I do if I was fearless ?**

✓ **What would I do if my love was unconditional ?**

We must allow the brain to anticipate the future in order to take off from the present.

PROGRAM TO INDUCE POSTURE AS THE ORIGIN OF **SELF-CONFIDENCE**

Changing the way to talk to others, and <u>to talk to ourselves</u>

Do you know that the subconscious mind is nonjudgmental?

Generally speaking, it is permeable to our own words. It is not opposed to our verbalization.

<u>**The subconscious doesn't even know the difference between «I» or «you» or «he/she».**</u>

So if you criticize others by saying, for example : " they **suck**», the subconscious will only remember the word "**suck**" and will probably apply it to you.

PART 2 INSTALLATION OF THE NEW OPERATING SYSTEM

<u>*It is accepted that everything returns to its source.*</u>

Thus every word that I say comes back to me sooner or later in the form of experiences.

AUTO-COACHING SOFTWARE

To become aware of your skills

" *A well-known lecturer* starts his seminar by holding up a 100 dollar bill.
He asks people : « Who would like to have that bill ? » The hands start to rise, so he says : « I'm going to give this 100 dollar bill to one of you, but first let me do something with it. » He then crumples the banknote with force and asks : « Do you still want that bill ? » Hands keep coming up. « Well, okay, but what happens if I do that ?» He throws the crumpled bill on the floor and jumps on it, crushing it as much as possible and covering it with dust from the floor.

Then he asks, « Who still wants that bill ? » Of course, the hands are still up!
« My friends, you have just learned a lesson... No matter what I do with this bill, you still want it because its value hasn't changed, it's still worth 100 dollars.

So think of yourself, of your life.
*Many times in your life you will be offended, rejected, soiled by people or events. You will feel like you are worthless but in reality your **intrinsic value won't be changed !** »*

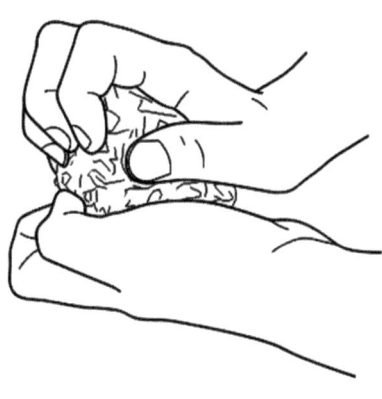

AUTO-COACHING SOFTWARE

To reduce stress

« *I'm thinking about the game and not about the stakes.* »

When the brain is fully focused on its purpose, it enables a state of mental and intellectual fluidity to be attained.

The power of concentration allows you to reach its maximum output.

Haven't you ever been so captivated by a book that you forgot to get off at the subway station?

The time you spend thinking about what's at stake, you don't spend it thinking about the game.

PART 2 SETTING UP OF THE NEW OPERATING SYSTEM

Example :

It's like a tennis player playing with a partner. Someone walks into the tennis court. Paralyzing thoughts arise : « What's he coming to do ? Is he coming to judge me ? Is he coming to recruit me ? Does he think I play well? Am I living up to his expectations?»

During this time, the player *is not focused on his game but on the stakes and his game starts to suffer.* He overplays or, on the contrary, misses his moves because he is no longer in the timing.

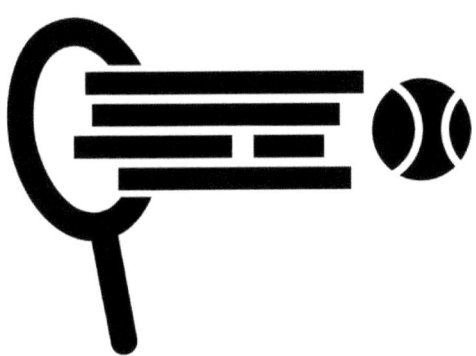

AUTO-COACHING SOFTWARE

To believe in your lucky star

"**There was** a very poor man in a village who had a very handsome...horse. The horse was so beautiful that the lords of the castle wanted to buy him...but the man was always refusing. « To me this horse is not an animal, it's a friend. How do you want me to sell a friend ? » he asked.

One morning he went to the stable and the horse was gone. All the villagers told him : « We told you so ! You'd better have sold it. Now it's stolen... what a bad luck ! » The old man says, « Luck, bad luck, who can tell ? »

Everybody's laughing at him. But 15 days later, the horse comes back, with a whole herd of wild horses. He had escaped, had seduced a beautiful mare and returned with the rest of the horde. « What luck ! » said the villagers.

The old man and his son started training wild horses. But a week later, his son breaks a leg in practice. « What bad luck ! » his friends say. « How are you going to do it, you who is already so...poor, if your son, your only support, can no longer help you ! »

PART 2 SETTING UP OF THE NEW OPERATING SYSTEM

The old man says, « Luck, bad luck, who can tell ? »

Some time later, the army of the lord of the country arrives in the village, and enlist by force all available young men. All of them... except the son of the old man...who has a broken leg.

«How lucky you are, all our children are gone off to war, and you're the only one keeping your son with you. Ours will maybe get killed...»

The old man says :

« Luck, bad luck, who can tell ? »

AUTO-COACHING SOFTWARE

For encouragement in all circumstances

To love oneself in all circumstances

Trust and esteem are one and the same.

Be gentle with yourself as your own caring coach.

Encourage yourself when you fail :

« Well done, you tried ! »
« I am proud of you. »
« Success is to go from failure to failure without losing your enthusiasm. » W. Churchill

PART 2 SETTING UP OF THE NEW OPERATING SYSTEM

To be inspiring

Accepting your own weaknesses

Be vulnerable - it will make you stronger !
You can inspire by making a mistake, it makes you more human. If the teacher forgets his words, you can tell yourself, that you too can allow yourself to do so.

A hero is always imperfect.

Example : every hero has an imperfection that allows us to recognize ourselves in him.

Superman's kryptonite, the Achilles heel, etc.

AUTO-COACHING SOFTWARE

To always look on the bright side

Focus on the wins

« *Either I win, or I learn, I never lose...* »
Nelson Mandela

The air we breathe is available to us without restriction. We accept this priceless gift, the most precious gift of our lives, without realizing it.

So why should we doubt the other gifts that are at our disposal ?

Our creative capacity is unlimited. Einstein claimed to use only 15% of his abilities.
It's up to you to discover, develop, and capitalize on it and let it nourish you.

Be grateful for what you have. If you focus on your lack of something, you run the risk of never digging yourself out of the hole.

PART 2 SETTING UP OF THE NEW OPERATING SYSTEM

AUTO-COACHING SOFTWARE

To develop self-awareness

Identify your strengths that justify selfconfidence

Everyone has a talent. What's yours?

Allow yourself to be proud of it !

At school, we often start from a perfect theoretical grade and subtract points for all the mistakes...

What a conditioning to break self-confidence!!!

It's time to change and focus on your strengths.

AUTO-COACHING SOFTWARE

To be zen

<u>We only take into account the present moment : we think neither of the past nor of the future</u>

The present is the only time that matters

Doesn't " present " also mean gift ?

PART 2 SETTING UP OF THE NEW OPERATING SYSTEM

SOFTWARE TO MAKE PEACE WITH YOUR FEARS

Perceive fear differently

The brain **is searching for pleasure at the same time it wants to avoid pain.**

To protect ourselves, we tend to see more of the loss than the gain.

HOWEVER

IT'S TIME TO MAKE PEACE WITH YOUR FEARS

If I'm living life, I really have to LIVE it.
The reality is that everything is balanced. There are as many « plusses » as « minuses ».
There are no more losses than gains.

PART 2 SETTING UP OF THE NEW OPERATING SYSTEM

Perceive fear differently

➤ **FEAR** is only a perception.

➤ **FEAR** is a manifestation that attacks us but at the same time protects us from danger.

➤ **FEAR** is also a biological phenomenon.

SOFTWARE TO MAKE PEACE WITH YOUR FEARS

Tame your fear of being judged...

To wonder what other people are going to think is a heavy burden to carry.
We live with a social mask in order to be loved.

The **self-confidence** can be easily built contrary to what we think.

How do you do it?

Create powerful affirmations and repeat them:

« I love being self-confident »

«I'm independent of the good or bad opinions of others »

PART 2 SETTING UP OF THE NEW OPERATING SYSTEM

" If I'm afraid of doing something, then I'm doing it ! "

The best way to fight fear is **ACTION.**

It's better to act right away than to accumulate a fear that prevents you from doing anything else because you think about it all the time.

Each time you are afraid to do something, **act**, because only action can relieve the pressure !

SOFTWARE TO MAKE PEACE WITH YOUR FEARS

To face and overcome one's fear

In order to face and overcome one's fear, it is necessary to confront the perception of the fear, and to respect it.

The following story illustrates this:

" **Three young Tibetan monks**, at the end of their years of apprenticeship, asked their old master what was the last test he had in store for them...before they could claim the name of wise men. Sitting in a tailor's suit in the small room where the master lived secluded, the three youngsters on the saw censers appear behind the smoke and listened quietly to what he had to say to them.
« Before you can reach the heights of wisdom, you must learn to endure loneliness. 100 days without seeing a living soul, alone in the desert. There's only one way to do that. It's up to you to discover it.»

PART 2 SETTING UP OF THE NEW OPERATING SYSTEM

The first monk did not really take this final test seriously. He had reason to believe that he could endure loneliness better than anyone else. « Loneliness is just a word, » he said, « and I only have to say it long enough to stop being afraid of it. » And he left with peace of mind for the desert.

The second monk, who had gone a little further in the study of wisdom, took some precautions : « Loneliness is not just a vain word, it is an idea, and it is this idea that is supposed to frighten us.
I must therefore reflect again and again on the meaning of loneliness so that I no longer fear it. »
He then immersed himself in books and, after a week of meditation, he felt ready for the desert.

The third monk, a discreet and perceptive young man who had been able to interpret the words of the old sage and to read between the lines of the texts he was given to study, prepared himself in a completely different way.

« He announced his departure long before the others, but even before reaching the desert, he got used to loneliness by staying in his cell and refusing visits.
He learned not to say a word all day and to fend for himself without relying on the help of others.

Finally, he left for the desert.

After a hundred days, the wise old man came out of retirement and looked at the horizon. He saw...a single monk appearing. The last one to leave. And the last to return because the first two had failed long before the end of the ordeal.

He greeted his pupil with these words :

" That's good. You are the only one who has looked loneliness in the face and entered into communion with it. You understood what it was by experiencing it and not by treating it as if it were just a word or an idea. You are now a wise man because you know that in order to face our fears we must not only face the opinion we have of the thing, but above all the thing directly. "

PART 2 SETTING UP OF THE NEW OPERATING SYSTEM

Fear is an opportunity to grow

SOFTWARE TO MAKE PEACE WITH YOUR FEARS

I allow myself the right to be afraid.

It's normal to be sensitive to the judgment of others.

Even the biggest stars have all felt an apprehension in front of other people's eyes.

<u>Do not try to suppress this fear because it will inhibit you. Instead, try to give yourself the right to be afraid. That will diminish its power over you.</u>

wanting to be loved → *wanting to inspire*

The more you're in control of what other people think, the more it takes up space into your life…

The less you are yourself,
the less you'll be accepted….

Rather than making a good impression
be yourself and express yourself !

Go from impression to expression

Focus on your goal

Wanting to be loved ? **NO**
Wanting to inspire ? **YES**

Confidence does not mean "not stressing". Confidence can mean inspiring someone; for instance - helping them to remember something, or motivating them to do something challenging or brand new that's never been done before.

If you think about yourself, the stress increases
***If you think about the others,
the stress decreases** !*

SOFTWARE TO MAKE PEACE WITH YOUR FEARS

Go from " Being " to " Doing "

Often when you are shy, you feel like everyone is watching and judging you. That everyone is waiting to see you stumble, hesitate, fail. It is because you are too focused on yourself, on your faults, on your supposed disabilities, and you think that everyone else is doing the same.

But people have lots of other things to do other than thinking of you.

Stop seeing people around you as if they had gathered in a special grand jury, just to evaluate you.

Instead of worrying about what people think of you, think about what you do for them.

PART 2 SETTING UP OF THE NEW OPERATING SYSTEM

PART 3

ANTIVIRUS SOFTWARE

After initializing our **operating system**,

we have set up a **new system** with multi-faceted perception program, program to make peace with our fears, program for auto-coaching, program to induce posture as the origin of **self-confidence**

All we have to do now is to set up **an anti-virus** to prevent the system from being infected with bad thoughts that destroy **self-confidence**

PART 3 ANTIVIRUS SOFTWARE

ALIGNMENT TWA

Thoughts
Words spoken
Acts

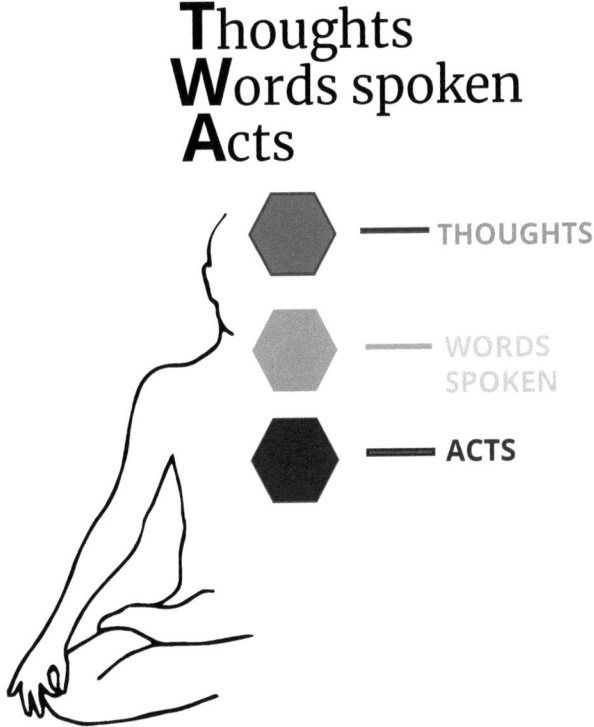

Antivirus program consists of properly aligning his thoughts, his words and his actions.

When you think well, you speak well, and then you act well. If one of its foundations deviates, it creates dissonance and therefore plays on **self-confidence;**

Example :
If you act badly (lie for example), you will live in dissonance, you will not be in harmony with yourself, so you will have negative thoughts and you may unconsciously get angry with yourself and others and therefore speak badly.

ALIGNMENT TWA

The antivirus works as an alert when one of the foundations of this alignment is deviating.

Example :
You catch yourself uttering bad words ?
→ **Tell yourself that you have to go back into alignment.**

Example :
You catch yourself making suppositions ?
→ **Tell yourself that you have to go back into alignment.**

THOUGHTS

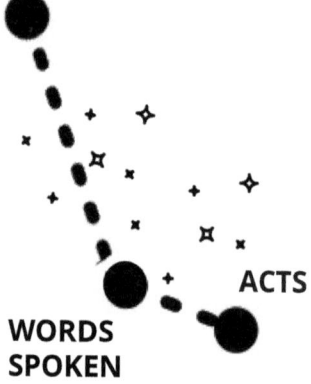

ACTS

WORDS SPOKEN

PART 3 ANTIVIRUS SOFTWARE

THOUGHTS FOR SELF-CONFIDENCE

Our thoughts condition our mind

We have thousands of thoughts a day. It is useless to add assumptions to these thoughts.
In 90% of the cases, those assumptions never come true. <u>So there is no point in making assumptions.</u>

This is **one of the Toltec chords** of Miguel RUIZ (the third one).

When you find yourself making assumptions, stop it because it is counterproductive.

THOUGHTS FOR SELF-CONFIDENCE

Our thoughts condition our mind

If you're not satisfied with your daily life,
don't dwell on it
or don't focus on what you don't want
in your life, but instead
focus on the things you really want.

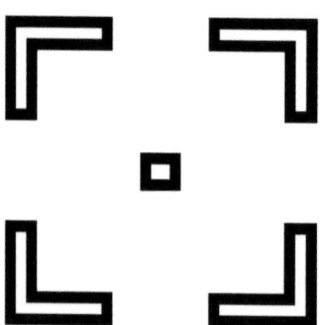

PART 3 ANTIVIRUS SOFTWARE

THOUGHTS FOR SELF-CONFIDENCE

Visualize the path, more than the goal

If you dream of making your plans come true, not only is it pleasurable, but you also condition your brain to project itself into the future.

The most important thing is not the realization of dreams, but the things you do to make them come true.

« To carry out your projects, Pretend you don't have another plan. »

There is a notorious book called « *The Art of War* » by Sun TZU.

It reveals the various techniques that a warlord must use in order to overthrow his enemy. The best strategy is to seek victory without death, without weapons and without confrontation.

According to Sun TZU, it's all in the suggestion.
In his book, Sun TZU explains that « *Soldiers who have no alternative but death, fight with the most savage energy. With nothing left to lose, they are no longer afraid; they don't give in an inch, since they have nowhere else to go.* » (chapter 11)

So, if you want to win the war, you must always leave a way out for people because in doing so, some will escape, others will hesitate.

Thus you create confusion.

PART 3 ANTIVIRUS SOFTWARE

<u>With the brain, it's the same as war.</u>

If you leave a way out in your brain and you say, « Come on, I'll do it, but in case it doesn't work, what do I do? You say to yourself : « *I'll do this, then I'll do this, this, or this !* »

What are you doing in your Brain?

The same thing Sun Tsu does in a village.
You create a rift that prevents you from fighting with the energy of desperation.

Once you set your goal, conquer it...

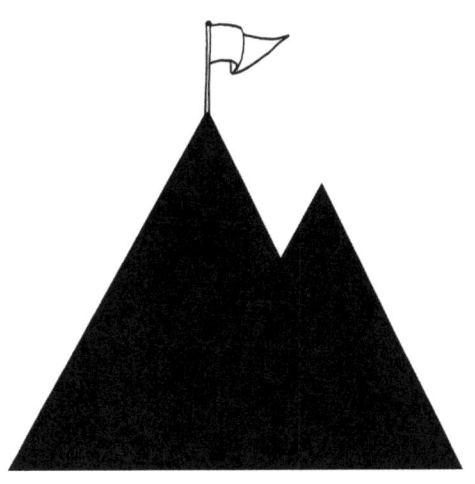

IMPECCABLE WORDS

Speaking positive conditions our unconscious

People who lack self-confidence tend to call each other names at the slightest misstep !
Stop insulting yourself, it destroys your **self-confidence.**
Have a kind word for yourself and others.
This is **the first teaching of the Toltec agreement.**
Remember that you are someone sensible, intelligent, reliable, and capable of beautiful things. Tell this to yourself as many times as necessary.
It's like watering a plant often to make it grow.

If you find yourself having a word that is not kind, pull yourself together and speak well !

PART 3 ANTIVIRUS SOFTWARE

ACT FOR TRUST

To gain more self-confidence, integrate these 6 simple principles :

- ✓ **RESPECT YOURSELF AND OTHERS**
  EVEN WHEN YOU DON'T UNDERSTAND THEM.
  DON'T TALK BEHIND PEOPLE'S BACKS.

- ✓ **BE RELIABLE** (SAY WHAT YOU ARE GOING TO DO AND DO WHAT YOU SAY)

- ✓ **BE HONEST** (TELL THE TRUTH)

- ✓ **DISTINGUISH WHAT YOU DO FROM WHAT YOU ARE**
  (DO NOT IDENTIFY YOURSELF WITH YOUR BEHAVIORS TO PREVENT DEPRECIATION IN CASE OF FAILURE)

- ✓ **DEFEND YOUR OPINIONS AND BELIEFS**

- ✓ **DO YOUR BEST**

CONCLUSION

CONCLUSION

You've come this far successfully !

You've successfully initialized the system that was crippling you in order to set up a new system that you can trust.

Enlarging your comfort zone is a daily job. It requires you to challenge yourself to dare a little bit more every day.

This book doesn't pretend to perfect your absolute confidence because human psychology is complex and dependent on immeasurable parameters. We are well aware of this.

However, this guide is intended to give you confidence before an event, whatever it may be.

Read it...Reread it and read it again...

It is sometimes useful, as for a computer, to reset the system when it crashes...

Being self-confident. That's what I wish for you with all my heart because this is the path that will lead us to the heights of success.

ACKNOWLEDGMENTS

I would like to tenderly thank my brother Lionel BOCHURBERG for his valuable advice. He lives in California and I miss him a lot.

I also wish to thank Mikhael KINLEY SAFRONOFF for the time he spent correcting the english translation of this book.

BIBLIOGRAPHY

Books :

CHEVALIER C/, *Faire face aux émotions*, Intereditions 2006
DE LASSUS R., *Oser être soi même*, Marabout 1992
DUCASSE F & CHAMALIDIS M., *Champion dans la tête*, Les éditions de l'homme 2004
BELLENGER L., *La confiance en soi*, Paris, ESF, 1987
FANGET F., *Oser*, *Thérapie de la confiance en soi*, Odile Jacob, 2003
PLUYETTE C., *Les secrets de la confiance en soi*, Management N°127, 2006
REGARD J., *Les émotions*, Eyrolles 2007
TZU SUN, *L'art de la guerre*, Hachette Pluriel Reference, 2015
BOCHURBERG A., *Le mental, clé de la performance*, Ed. Cithéa, 2010
RUIZ M. *Les quatre accords toltèques, la voie de la liberté personnelle* Ed. Jouvence, Poches , 2016
MERLEAU-PONTY M., *Phénoménologie de la perception*, Ed. Gallimard, 1976
BOCHURBERG C., *Parole au corps*, Ed. L'Harmattan, 2004
BURTON K., N. PLATTS B., *Booster sa confiance en soi pour les Nuls*, Ed. First, 2018

Websites :

https://www.macreationdentreprise.fr/confiance-en-soi/, *confiance en soi : 10 trucs infaillibles pour la développer*, By Antonella, posté le 14 octobre 2016
https://hypnose-ericksonienne.com/fr/a-consulter/contes-et-histoires/